# The Spirit of André
### The story of a little dog with a big heart

**Farnaz Zirakbash**
Illustrated by Tristan Tait

To order more copies, or to contact the author,
visit www.vividpublishing.com.au / thespiritofandre

Copyright © 2024 Farnaz Zirakbash

ISBN: 978-1-923078-24-6 (hardcover edition)
Published by Vivid Publishing
A division of Fontaine Publishing Group
P.O. Box 948, Fremantle
Western Australia 6959
www.vividpublishing.com.au

 A catalogue record for this book is available from the National Library of Australia

All rights reserved. No part of this publication may be reproduced, stored in a retrieval system or transmitted in any form or by any means, electronic, mechanical, photocopying, recording or otherwise, without the prior written permission of the copyright holder.

In memory of my sweet little André who, despite facing various health challenges, lived a life which was an inspiration to all who knew him.

*"Goodbyes are only for those who love with their eyes. Because for those who love with heart and soul there is no such thing as separation."*
*– Rumi, Persian poet*

My name is André. My fur is very curly and in winter, when it is long, I look like a fluffy ball of wool.

I am 14 years old and live with my mum in an adorable apartment with a little courtyard.

I love my life so much. My days are filled with joyful adventures and my tail is always wagging.

When I was very little my leg was broken. So now my front left leg has a special plate in it that helps me play and run like other dogs.

I have a special routine that I follow every day.

I get up very early and have breakfast at 5am. Eating on time is important for my health.

I love my food so much that sometimes I try to trick my mum. I wake her at 3am and tell her it's time for breakfast. But my mum is so clever and says, "It's too early, André. Go back to sleep."

I try again at 3.30 and again at 4 but my mum does not budge. Finally, when it is truly 5am, she gets up and feeds me. I wonder how she always knows what time it is?

I have a condition called diabetes which means my body needs a little extra care. I've had this condition since I was 5 years old. After breakfast I need an injection to keep my blood sugar balanced throughout the day.

When my belly is full, I go back to sleep until 9am and then my mum takes me for a walk. I love my morning walks and smile all the way.

My mum changes our walks all the time to make them exciting and challenging for me and I enjoy sniffing new areas along the way. But there are a few routes that are my absolute favourites and my mum knows them well.

There is something about me that makes me even more special. I am blind. But not being able to see doesn't stop me from enjoying my walks. There's still lots to sniff and explore.

My mum takes great care of me so I never bump into anything — she stays right by my side and guides me safely. I trust my mum and can sense her presence. I know she will keep me out of harm's way so I happily stroll along and cherish every moment.

Because of my age, it doesn't take much for me to get tired so after my morning walk I mostly sleep till the afternoon when I go outside and sit near the gate. When other dogs pass by, I chase them along the fence and bark with joy. I love this game. It is so much fun.

Some days my mum leaves home after our morning walk. I don't know where she goes but before she leaves, a kind person comes to look after me. Her name is Amy. I love Amy and enjoy playing with her, but I miss my mum and eagerly wait all day for her. I know she always comes home just before my dinner time.

At 5pm, after my meal and second injection, my mum takes me for another walk. We choose a different path to the morning and both enjoy the peacefulness of the evening. When we're home, I curl up in my cosy bed and drift into sweet dreams. Before bedtime, my mum showers me with kisses and cuddles, and pats me until I fall asleep.

For the last two years I haven't been able to hear my mum's voice. Being deaf is my other special quality. It allows me to experience the world around me in a very unique way. Although I cannot hear my mum, I know she is telling me how much she loves me when she gently tickles my fluffy belly and kisses me.

I miss hearing my mum's voice but love is not something that needs words or sounds; it is felt deeply in your heart. I feel the warmth and affection of my mum, and my nose is blessed with the ability to smell love.

One evening everything changes. I have no appetite and nothing tempts me to eat. My mum is so worried and we go to the vet.

The vet takes my blood and does some tests to find out the cause of my sickness. I eat a little food the next day just to make my mum happy but I no longer love my food and have no interest in going for a walk or to sit at the gate and chase other dogs. I'm tired all the time. All I want is to be in my mum's arms and to smell her comforting presence.

Days turn to weeks and I do not feel better. My appetite for food does not return and I no longer have any interest in playing. During this time I sense my mum's love that is always there and she does not leave my side.

One night while sleeping in my mum's arms something magical happens. I find myself in a beautiful place filled with other dogs, lots of toys and plenty of food. I suddenly have lots of energy again and want to run, just like when I was a pup.

What is this place? I wonder. But something is very strange. Where is my mum? I search for her everywhere but cannot find her. Will she return before dinner time?

I love being in this beautiful place, running and playing with joy. But I miss my mum so much. I'll never forget her, and I know she will never forget me. Our love is always in our hearts. Deep down I know we will be reunited again one day when the time is right.

Even though I am not by my mum's side anymore, my spirit still dances around her heart bringing warmth, love, and happy memories whenever she thinks of me.

Remember, even if a pet faces health challenges or things that make their life a bit different, they can still have the happiest time ever with their loving family by their side. No matter what, love can always make every day a big, joyful adventure!

## ABOUT THE AUTHOR

Farnaz Zirakbash made the journey from Iran to Australia in 2007, without family of her own. A risk-taker, she began her Australian journey washing dishes, eventually forging a path to earn a doctorate in sociology and became a university lecturer and an Australian citizen. Amidst her accomplishments, Farnaz found profound joy and love when she adopted André, a courageous little dog whose health challenges inspired her to write her first children's book "The Trouble with André".

*Here is the author with her dog, Shadow*

Now, Farnaz has a new dog companion named "Shadow," who has a remarkable resemblance to André. As the shadow of André, this new little dog has brought immense joy to Farnaz's life, and Farnaz adores him just as she did André. The spirit of André appears to guide and watch over Shadow, creating a heartwarming connection.

Farnaz exclusively writes narratives centered around animals, conveying a powerful message about the transformative influence of love. The author's true stories of the transforming magic of love will inspire families who are facing the challenge of children or pets who are sick.

**To order more copies, or to contact the author, visit www.vividpublishing.com.au / thespiritofandre**

Milton Keynes UK
Ingram Content Group UK Ltd.
UKHW050653250424
441570UK00003BA/60

9 781923 078246